What's the Time?

Nicolas Brasch

Rigby®

www.Rigby.com
1-800-531-5015

Rigby Focus Forward

This Edition © 2009 Rigby, a Harcourt Education Imprint

Published in 2006 by Nelson Australia Pty Ltd ACN: 058 280 149
A Cengage Learning company

1 2 3 4 5 6 7 8 374 14 13 12 11 10 09 08 07
Printed and bound in China

What's the Time
ISBN-13   978-1-4190-3680-4
ISBN-10   1-4190-3680-7

Acknowledgments
Illustrations by Gaston Vanzet
The author and publisher would like to acknowledge permission to reproduce material
from the following sources:
Photographs by Bill Thomas/ Imagen, p. 5; Istockphoto.com/ Louis Aguinaldo, p. 4 inset;
NASA Images, pp. 8, 10, 12-13; PhotoDisc/ Getty Royalty Free/ Harcourt Index, p. 5;
Photos.com, p. 4.

What's the Time?

Nicolas Brasch

Contents

Measuring Time

Time can be **measured** in hours, minutes, and seconds.

April

Monday	Tuesday	Wednesday	Thursday	Friday
				1
4	5	6	7	8
11	12	13	14	15
18	19	20	21	22	23	24
25	26	27	28	29	30

February

Sunday	Monday	Tuesday	Wednesday	Thursday	Friday	Saturday
1	2	3	4	5	6	7
8	9	10	11	12	13	14
15	16	17	18	19	20	21
22	23	24	25	26	27	28

Time can also be measured in days, weeks, months, and years.

Parts of Time

Time is made up of parts.

2. There are 60 minutes in an hour.

1. There are 60 seconds in a minute.

6. There are 12 months in a year.

3. There are 24 hours in a day.

4. There are 7 days in a week.

May
Monday 23

Tuesday 24

Wednesday 25

May
Thursday 26

Friday 27

Saturday 28   Sunday

MAY
23
WEEK 22

5. There are 52 weeks in a year.

Measuring a Year

Earth

moon

A year is measured by how long it takes
for Earth to go around the sun.
It takes 365 days for Earth to go around the sun.
There are 365 days in one year.

un

So it takes one year for Earth to go all the way around the sun.

Measuring a Month

In the past, people measured time by the moon.

The moon goes around Earth. The time it takes for the moon to go around Earth is called a month.

moon

It takes the moon 29.5 days
to go all the way around Earth.

But we cannot have 29.5 days in a month.
So February has 28 days, or 29 days if it is a **leap year**.
The rest of the months have 30 or 31 days.

sun

Earth

Measuring a Day

Earth spins around.

The time it takes for Earth to spin all the way around is what we call a day.

day

It is day when the parts of Earth that we live in face the sun.

It is night when the parts of Earth we live in do not face the sun.

night

Measuring Time in the Past

In the past, time was measured by different **instruments**.

One of the first instruments to measure time was the **sundial**.

Time is measured by where the sun's shadow falls on the sundial.

A sundial has marks for all the hours.
When the sun is right over a sundial, the time is 12:00.

Glossary

instruments	things used for measuring
leap year	a year that has 366 days. Leap years are every four years.
measured	worked out the amount of something
sundial	an instrument that shows, or measures, time

Index